D1561153

KAROL
The Boy Who Became Pope

A Story about Saint John Paul II

WRITTEN BY **Jem Sullivan**

ILLUSTRATED BY **William J. Maloney**

NEUMANN PRESS

A Special Gift for

_____

from

Acknowledgements

Saint Benedict, in his well known Rule, urges that, "whatever good work you begin to do, beg of God with most earnest prayer to perfect it." So I wish to thank God, first of all, in whose grace this work began and was brought to completion. I wish to thank the talented editorial team at Neumann Press for their enthusiasm, commitment to excellence, and their professionalism. And I am indebted to William J. Maloney, for his willingness to collaborate on this project. He is an exceptional artist and a sheer delight to work with.

Above all, I am deeply grateful to my husband, Scott, for his unfailing support, constant prayers, and love that makes so much possible.

Author's Note

Karol: The Boy Who Became Pope is a story about the childhood of Saint John Paul II. While based on historical events, certain elements have been fictionalized.

Published in the United States by
Neumann Press
PO Box 410487
Charlotte, NC 28241
www.NeumannPress.com
1-800-437-5876

Printed in the United States by
Bookmasters, Inc., 30 Amberwood
Parkway, Ashland, OH 44805
Job number 50003809. May 2014.

Text © 2014 Jem Sullivan.

Illustrations © 2014 William J. Maloney.

Dedication

This book is dedicated to my son, Benedict,
on his First Holy Communion.

KAROL

The Boy Who Became Pope

In the beautiful and ancient country of Poland, in the town of Wadowice, lived a boy named Karol. His family and friends called him "Lolek."

Karol loved new adventures. As a boy he played with his friends, helped his neighbors, and prayed with his family. When he grew up he became a priest, a bishop, and a beloved pope.

The story you are about to read will take you on a few adventures with Karol, the boy who would one day become a great saint of the Church.

Are you ready to join Karol on his adventures?

Karol was named after his father. Mister Wojtyła was an army officer who worked in Wadowice. His friends called him "Captain." He was a quiet and kind man who loved his family. His faith in God was deep and strong.

Emilia, Karol's mother, was proud of her sons. Edmund was Karol's older brother. He wanted to be a doctor when he grew up.

"Do you need help, Mama?" asked Karol. It was a late summer afternoon and his mother was busy preparing a delicious meal. The whole family had worked around the house that day. Now their home seemed to sparkle.

"Yes, Lolek," his mother replied with a smile, as she gently wiped her forehead, "please open the windows. The house is getting a bit too warm with all the cooking."

The Wojtyla family lived in a small apartment, not far from the Church of Saint Mary. In fact, they were so close that they could hear the church bells ring on the hour. The music of the bells reminded them of God —His presence, protection, and love.

As Karol opened wide the windows a light breeze fluttered the lace curtains around his face. And instantly the gentle chimes of church bells filled the small living room.

"Ding! Dong!" "Ding! Dong!" "Ding! Dong!"

Evening prayers were about to begin. Soon waves of music carried these words of prayer from the church right into the heart of their home.

"For He who is mighty has done great things for me, and holy is His name!" (Luke 1: 49)

The Church of Saint Mary was the center of life in the town of Wadowice. The Wojtyła home was simple and lively. It was filled with many sounds— laughter, talking, reading, music, singing, and prayer.

"Your birthday is coming soon, isn't it?" asked Karol's father.

Karol was born on the eighteenth day of May, the month of the Virgin Mary. It was in the year 1920. His birth was a time of great joy for his family.

In Poland, a great war had just ended. There was peace again. During the month of May, in every town and village in Poland, children brought beautiful crowns of flowers to Mary, the mother of Jesus. Some towns celebrated with festivals, processions, and fairs in honor of Mary.

Each year, the Wojtyła family joined in the May procession as the town prayed and sang to the Virgin Mary.

"I've been thinking about this for a while," Karol's father continued, as the family sat around the dinner table. "How would you like to go on a family pilgrimage this summer? It will be a short trip but I am sure it will be packed with spiritual blessings and some fun adventures."

"I would love to do that!" said Karol's mother, as she carried a bowl of steaming potato soup to the table.

"And so would I!" shouted Karol excitedly, "and where would we go?"

"Oh, yes!" said Edmund, "and when can we go?" His voice filled with excitement as he added, "I just went on a field trip to the salt mine with my classmates. I love to see new places."

"Well," said their father, "Karol turns eight in a few weeks and next year he will receive First Holy Communion. So I thought we might celebrate his birthday with a family pilgrimage. It will also help Karol prepare to receive Jesus on that special day."

Karol looked forward to his First Holy Communion Day.

He remembered when his mother joined his baby hands in prayer and taught him to make the sign of the Cross—in the name of the Father, and of the Son, and of the Holy Spirit.

"Did anyone happen to see our newest neighbor, baby Adam? His mother Anna walked by our house this morning?" asked Karol's mother.

"Oh yes, I did," replied Mister Wojtyła, "and what a precious gift of new life he is. Seeing him made me think back to when your mother would take you both for a walk in the neighborhood. She never missed a chance to say to our friends, "I know one day my sons will be great!"

"Life is a precious gift from God," said Karol's mother as she turned to her sons. "And because life comes from

God, the Creator of the world, everyone is a child of God with great dignity."

Karol never forgot his mother's words.

When he was a baby Karol delighted neighbors and friends with his lively face, intelligent eyes, and playful smile. If a priest happened to pass by when they walked across town his mother always asked for a blessing on her son.

Karol grew to be a strong, talented, and kind young boy.

The Wojtyla family enjoyed walking through the town market and square, called the Rynek. After Sunday Mass and on special feasts days they stopped at the local bakery.

"We have some extra cream cakes for Mrs. Belinski," said Emilia, "could you please take them to her, Karol?" Mrs. Belinski was an elderly neighbor.

Karol was building a small fortress. He and his friend Jerzy were about to play a game of make-believe battles when they imagined they were great Polish heroes.

"Sure, mother, I'll take them to her right away."

Karol knew that Mrs. Belinski liked visitors. She lived alone after losing most of her family during the war. He slipped on his shoes quickly and ran out of the house. The freshly baked treats wobbled gently in the white cake box that he held tightly in his hands.

Faint music echoed in the narrow stairs to Mrs. Belinski's apartment. She spent most of her day playing the piano. Beautiful music, she liked to say, was her friend and companion.

"Hello, Mrs. Belinski, it's me again," said Karol, as he knocked

gently on her door. He had run so fast that he was out of breath now.

"Oh, you are a kind boy," the old lady said softly at the door. "Are you out of school for the summer already? How is your family? And how are your friends?"

She opened the box and the scent of warm cakes instantly filled the room. The simple gift brought a smile to her wrinkled face and a twinkle to her tired eyes.

"Come in and let me play you my favorite piece by our great composer, Chopin," she said. Karol sat in a big old armchair and leaned back to listen. Sweet notes slowly filled the room. It was a concert just for him!

"Thank you, that was lovely. But I should leave now," Karol said. "It's almost dinner time."

Mrs. Belinski stood up from her piano and shuffled across the room. She took one tiny treat from a candy jar and placed it in Karol's hand. It was her small way of saying "thank you!"

Every Thursday the town square became a lively place where neighbors shopped, talked, or simply relaxed. The children played in the open square in front of the market stalls. There were many shops where one could find almost everything—from fresh flowers to vegetables and meats, bicycles and games, and pots and pans painted with brightly colored flowers!

The children loved the bakery and the ice cream shops that stood side by side. As they played in the open square, the whiff of warm bread seemed to pull the children close to the doors.

When they ran past the ice cream shop the children looked in the window to see if their favorite flavors—vanilla, strawberry, and chocolate—were in the colorful display!

Summer was the most adventurous time of the year for Karol and his friends. They would meet, play, and read old and new stories. The fields were green, flowers bloomed everywhere, and it seemed that everyone was just a bit more relaxed. Summer days seemed longer and Karol and Edmund would stay up a little later than usual.

"I'll be down at the field for goalie practice," said Karol to his mother. He was proud to be the goalkeeper of his class soccer team.

At home, his father and brother played simple games, like ping-pong on the kitchen table, and soccer in the living room with a ball made of rags. A few summers before, Karol learned to swim in the Skawa river. When winter came, he played hockey in a nearby field.

Most of all, Karol loved to ski. Each time he raced down the slopes the rush of crisp cold air and the shower of snow spraying his face was an adventure in itself.

17

"Could we read the story of Saint Stanisław, the Martyr?" Karol asked one evening.

"Sure, son," replied his father, "why don't you pick the book you'd like to read after dinner."

Mister Wojtyła enjoyed reading with his children. It was one of their favorite family activities. Sometimes they chose books about the history of Poland and stories of brave heroes. At other times, they read about the faith and lives of Polish saints and martyrs.

Karol had heard the story of Saint Stanisław before. He was a holy man of virtue who lived some nine hundred years ago, during the reign of King Boleslaw. He was known for his faith and courage when he became the beloved bishop of Kraków. When the king disobeyed God's commands the bishop spoke out loud. Eventually, he was killed by the king in the year 1079.

Karol listened carefully as his father began to read. He moved a bit closer when they came to the end of the story. It was the moment when Bishop Stanisław was celebrating Mass and the angry king rushed in to kill him. In life and in death, this holy bishop was a true friend of God.

Karol knew he wanted to be like him, strong in faith and in love of God.

At the end of summer it would be time to return to school. Karol loved his school—the Wadowice School. There he would meet classmates, see old friends, and make new friends too. He looked forward to the first day of school.

But before that an unforgettable adventure was waiting for Karol. He and his family would go on pilgrimage to Ludźmierz.

"We better start packing soon," said Emilia to her sons. Karol's father nodded in agreement as he put a few bread rolls leftover from lunch into a bag. Then he and Edmund folded a large camping tent into an old green backpack.

"Let's not be late. Our train leaves at seven o'clock this evening," he said.

Karol began searching for his grey backpack. He had been reading a book of short poems but now he could not remember where he put it. As he scanned the bookshelf a small yellow notebook fell to the floor. He opened it and was delighted to see many empty pages still there. It would be a perfect place to write about and draw his adventures.

So into his backpack went the notebook, poetry book and some clothes. And even though his backpack had filled up he had a feeling he was forgetting something. Soon the family would be ready to leave.

"I know we've been on pilgrimage before. But what is a pilgrimage?" asked Karol. He heard his mother and father talking about the beautiful shrines of Poland. But he was younger then. Now he was older and ready for this adventure.

"That's a good question, Karol," said Mister Wojtyła, as he sat down at the table.

"Since all that exists comes from the loving hand of God," he continued with a gentle smile, "there is no place on earth where God cannot be found.

In fact, God is present in every corner of the earth. The whole world is like a great sanctuary of His presence."

Both boys turned to listen as their father leaned forward, lowered his face, and looked out gently over his glasses, just as he did whenever he had something important to say.

"There are, however, certain places that are sacred and holy, because God is present there in a special way. These holy places bear the stamp of God's presence through Mary, his Blessed Mother, or through the life of a saint of the Church."

"Like the holy ground that Moses walked on when he saw the burning bush?" asked Edmund.

"Exactly!" said Mister Wojtyła, "in the Bible, mountains are places of mystery. There was Mount Sinai where Moses received the holy name of God, and the sign of his powerful presence in the burning bush. There also he received the Ten Commandments of God's law, which was the presence of God among the people of Israel. And then on Mount Nebo, Moses looked at the Promised Land with eyes filled with hope and gratitude to God."

He turned to close his overstuffed bag, now bursting with clothes and the family camping tent. It barely closed so he stood up and pressed the old suitcase down with one hand, while Edmund locked it.

Then he continued saying, "The Bible tells us that God's most perfect presence in the world is in His Son, Jesus. He "pitched his tent" among us, as the Gospel of John says. At the heart of every church or shrine is Jesus himself. There His real presence continues in the world."

The Wadowice train station was a busy place, bustling with movement. The large main hall of the train station was the center of much activity. As travelers entered or left the station, they glanced quickly at the large wooden clock above the entrance to the train platform.

The station clock kept perfect time. It sat in a beautiful carved dark wooden frame. The clock was so large that one could watch the hands move, inch by inch, around the clock face.

Below the giant clock were the ticket window and the train schedule board. On the left there were "ARRIVALS" and on the right were "DEPARTURES." People lingered in front of the schedule board.

Karol looked at the board carefully till he saw the train that would take them to the town near Ludźmierz. It was train number 78.

At the center of the station hall were two rows of small shops selling newspapers, snacks, and flowers. Around the edge of the main hall were long wooden benches with metal curved arms. They were beautifully carved too but worn down by travelers coming and going every day. It seemed like the wooden benches were the only things that did not move at the train station.

"Look," said Karol pointing across the station hall, "I think I see Marta and her family here."

Marta was a friend of Karol. They had performed in a short play during the awards assembly at the end of the school year.

"Hello, Karol," said Marta, as she ran over to greet him. "Where are you going today?"

"We're going on pilgrimage," he replied. "And what about you, are you leaving too?"

"We're going to visit my grandparents who live near the Tatra mountains. And I can't wait to see my cousins there too!" she said excitedly, swinging her backpack from side to side.

Marta had a fresh red flower pinned to her hair. It was the same color as her curly red hair.

As soon as he saw the flower in Marta's hair, Karol remembered what he had almost forgotten! He meant to bring flowers to offer to the Mother of God at the shrine of Ludźmierz.

He waved goodbye to Marta and her family. Then he ran quickly to his father and said, "Could I buy a flower for our Blessed Mother?"

"Oh, sure son," said his father, as he searched his jacket pockets. "Here you go, and make sure you buy one for each of us," he added, as he placed four small coins in Karol's hand.

The station clock was at six fifty-five now and the train to Ludźmierz would arrive soon. As the family walked onto the platform they could see train number 78 moving into the station. The old engine puffed and steamed till it came to a creaky stop.

The Wojtyłas were just in time to begin their pilgrimage.

"All aboard," said the train conductor, in a booming voice. He greeted passengers with a smile. He had large, strong hands, like those of men who work with their hands all day.

The sun was about to set as the train pulled out of the station. The blue summer sky was a dazzling canvas painted with long streaks of twilight colors of orange, purple, and fading gold.

"Look! Is there anything more beautiful?" said Emilia to her husband and sons, as they looked out of the train window. "God, the Divine Artist is at work again!" she added with a smile.

The train began to pick up speed. Soon towns and villages, farms and cattle, fields and pine trees along winding country roads appeared and faded quickly before their eyes. Every now and then a small roadside shrine or old wayside cross could be seen in the pale twilight.

The Wojtyła family settled into a small compartment with sturdy wooden benches. Karol and Edmund sat in two opposite window seats. There would be a few stops before their destination.

Mister Wojtyła pulled the daily newspaper out of his bag and handed his wife a few pages. At first, Karol and Edmund talked excitedly about everything they saw. Eventually, the steaming sound of the engine and the clanging of the wheels below them lulled everyone into silence.

The fields were fresh after spring rains turned the cold earth into a floor of warm grass. A faint line of mountains could be seen in the far distance. By now Karol was busy drawing and writing in his yellow notebook. All that he saw from the train window was a reminder of the presence and love of God, Creator of the world, and the source of true beauty.

Excuse me, are these seats empty?" asked a young man. Close behind him were his wife and young daughter. She was about three years old.

"Yes, please take a seat," said Karol's father, "there is plenty of room for all of us."

The family squeezed into the small compartment. Along with their bags they carried musical instruments—two violins and a small tambourine.

"Where are you going?" said Emilia to the mother of the family. "Well," the lady replied, "we are musicians and we are going to play in a music festival in the mountains. It takes place every year during the summer harvest." Then she asked, "And you? Is your family on vacation?

The two women continued talking. In the meantime, the little girl stretched forward to look out of the window. Suddenly she began to cry. It began in small sniffles and ended in a loud sob.

"What's the matter, Anna?" asked her mother, as she turned in surprise. "Why do you cry?"

"I would like a flower just like that one," said the little girl, sobbing and pointing to Karol.

He looked down at the flower pinned onto his jacket. It was the one he had bought at the train station to offer to Mary, the Mother of Jesus.

"Here you go. You may have this flower," Karol said, as he reached out to the little girl. She was smiling now. "You will enjoy its fragrance and color for a long time," Karol added.

"Thank you so much," said the girl's mother to Karol. "You are so kind. For your generosity we would like to play a folk song for all of you?"

The little girl held the tambourine in her tiny hands, while her parents tuned their violins.

Soon the train was filled with the happy sounds of a lively Polish folksong.

Nowy Targ was the nearest train station to Ludźmierz. The sun had set and it was dark when the Wojtyła family stepped off the train into the mountain village.

They would spend the night in the town campground. Then the next morning they would take the first bus to Ludźmierz. As they walked from the station to the campground they were joined by other travelers looking for places to rest that night.

"This looks like a good spot to camp," said Mister Wojtyła, as they reached the edge of a small forest. A stream ran along the short pine trees. Edmund lit two small oil lanterns while Karol helped his father with the tent. Then they prepared a small fire outside the tent.

Karol's mother took out cold sandwiches and fresh pickles she had prepared for dinner. From her bag also came some apples and pears. She scooped a little water from the stream into a small cup to hold the flowers that Karol had bought at the train station.

The family gathered around the small sparkling fire. Their faces radiated a warm golden light. The food was cold but they were warm from the joy of being together.

"Oh, was I hungry!" said Karol's father at the end of the meal. "You know this mountain air is good for you. It makes one strong."

They could feel crisp cold air spread across the campground. A few bright stars twinkled as they peeked out from white clouds in the dark blue sky.

"What was that noise?" said Karol, half turned toward the pine trees. His eyes widened as he listened again for a strange sound that seemed to come from the direction of the forest. The mountain woods were home to some wild animals and they could be heard from the campsite.

"I'm scared!" said Karol, as he inched a bit closer to his father and mother. "Are there bears in the woods? What about snakes? Or mountain lions?" he asked. "Do you think we'll be safe sleeping so close to the forest in the dark?" he added, with his eyes still wide open.

"Do not be afraid, my son," said his father in a deep voice that gently crackled over the sparks of fire darting around their faces. "When you give your life to God you need not be afraid of anything or any person. Who knows what will happen to our country if there is a second war. But whatever comes our way should fill us with strength and love, not fear. For God is with us always."

"Yes," said his mother, as she pulled Karol close to her face. "You have no need to fear anything or anyone. Take your fears and place them in the hands of Jesus, Mary, his Mother, and Joseph. And remember, we are on pilgrimage. God is nearer to us than we can see or imagine. Our whole life is like a pilgrimage and God walks with us every day."

"**It's getting late.** I think it's time for night prayer," said Edmund.

"Good idea!" said his father. The family huddled close around the fire. Then they reached out to join hands in prayer.

"Our help is in the name of the Lord," said Karol's father, as he began to pray.

His family replied, "Who made heaven and earth!"

Karol looked out over the dark forest and the mighty mountains. Deep in his soul he felt the presence and grandeur of God.

"Night holds no terror for me sleeping under God's wings," continued his father, as he recited, from memory, the words of Psalm 91.

"He who dwells in the shelter of the Most High and abides in the shadow of the Almighty says to the Lord: "My refuge, my stronghold, my God, in whom I trust!"

The Wojtyła family continued praying words that were familiar from their night prayers at home.

But now in this mountain place of peace, beauty, and mystery, the prayer came to life in a new way.

"You will not fear the terror of the night nor the arrow that flies by day, nor the plague that prowls in the darkness nor the scourge that lays waste

at noon… For you has He commanded his angels, to keep you in all your ways, They shall bear you upon their hands, lest you strike your foot against a stone, On the lion and the viper you will tread, and trample the young lion and the dragon."

Karol's mother continued praying the next verse of the psalm.

"When he calls I shall answer: 'I am with you.' I will save him in distress and give him glory, With length of life I will content him; I shall let him see my saving power."

All at once, the four of them bowed their heads toward the light from the fire that was slowly fading.

"Glory be to the Father, and to the Son, and to the Holy Spirit: as it was in the beginning, is now, and ever shall be, world without end. Amen."

The last flames of the campfire faded out. In the stillness of the night they shuffled quietly into their tent, after saying good night to each other. Soon the whole family was falling asleep.

It was pitch dark now. Karol could see a few bright stars through the tent opening. A light rain was falling over the camp. And strange distant sounds of unknown mountain creatures could still be heard.

But Karol was not afraid.

Tweet-tweet, chirp-chirp, tweet-tweet. Songbirds greeted campers the next morning.

The night rain had stopped and bright rays of sunlight climbed the mountains slowly. Not a cloud was in sight. It was a perfect day to be on pilgrimage.

"If we're going to catch the first bus we'll need to hurry," said Emilia, as she put some bread rolls and slices of cheese on a plate.

After breakfast they took turns to wash in the nearby stream. The mountain water was cool and clean. It was like liquid silver.

As Karol knelt down to wash his hands and face in the stream he was reminded of the waters of Baptism. He thought of his catechism teacher, Father Zacher, who reminded the children that, "Faith is a gift from God that begins in the waters of Baptism. The first gift of faith in Jesus is given once in Baptism. But then Jesus comes to us over and over and over again in the Eucharist."

The bus ride to Ludźmierz would be a short trip on a winding mountain road. Mister Wojtyła talked excitedly to his family, who was squeezed into the narrow bus seats.

"Soon we will pray before the Mother of God of Ludźmierz. It is an ancient and miraculous statue that is about six hundred years old," he said to Karol.

"Is it true that they also call her the Shepherdess of Podhale?" asked Karol's mother.

"Oh, yes," replied his father. "That name comes from an old story about a wandering trader who got lost in the swampy forest of the mountains. The Mother of Jesus came to him and guided him to the church. As he knelt down to say "thank you" to Mary, a miraculous spring bubbled out of the ground."

"Look," said Karol in a voice bursting with excitement, as he pointed to the church spire that could be seen from afar. "We're almost there!"

The bus drove past the Ludźmierz town center and a few small shops—a bakery, a fish market, and a ski store. In the window Karol could see many skis in all sizes and bright colors.

As the bus turned onto the church road the sound of steeple bells echoed across the fields.

They had arrived just in time for Mass that was about to begin.

"ALL GUESTS WHO PRESENT THEMSELVES
ARE TO BE WELCOMED AS CHRIST."

Karol read aloud the large entrance sign that greeted pilgrims. A long time ago Cistercian monks had cared for this shrine. The monks were followers of Saint Benedict who taught them that to welcome a visitor was to welcome Jesus himself.

From the entrance a winding road lead to the church. Pilgrims in small and large groups walked ahead and behind Karol and his family. Some held rosaries. Others prayed on their knees.

"Ave, Ave, Ave, Maria! Ave, Ave, Maria!"

As they neared the church, pilgrims softly hummed the hymn that could be heard from afar.

"Immaculate Mary, your praises we sing! You reign now in splendor with Jesus our King!"

The hymn got louder and louder, as the music echoed against the stone walls of the church.

"Ave, Ave, Ave, Maria! Ave, Ave, Maria!"

"Welcome to this shrine of the Mother of God," said the old priest who stood at the church entrance. As he repeated this greeting to passing pilgrims, his rosary beads moved continuously through his fingers.

As Karol and his family walked by they could hear him say, "Today, we are blessed to have a visiting priest, Father Adam. He is a monk from a nearby Cistercian monastery."

Then he looked at Karol and Edmund and said, "Be sure to listen carefully to Father Adam."

Then he smiled and added, "Near the main altar you'll see a large wooden box filled with rosaries, just like this one!"

He held up his brown wooden rosary for everyone to see.

"Every child who visits this shrine receives one of these," he said.

"But there are also a few rare ones in that large box," he added. "But we never know when or who will get a special rosary."

After the opening prayers of Mass and the Bible readings, the old monk climbed the high pulpit to preach. He spoke in a soft, slow voice that was filled with wisdom and prayer.

"Our holy father, Saint Bernard once said that there are three comings of our Lord," he began.

Karol leaned forward to listen. "Three comings of Jesus," he thought. "How could that be?"

"In his first coming," the monk continued, "Jesus came to earth to walk, talk, and live among us. In his final coming we will see him in majesty and in bright glory. But now," he paused, "now is the time of his middle coming. And if our hearts and minds are open then Jesus comes to us even now in the love of those around us."

Then he pointed to the altar and said, "And every time the Church celebrates the Eucharist we welcome Jesus who comes to dwell among us."

Karol was moved by his simple words. He was beginning to understand the great gift he would receive at First Holy Communion.

Then the old monk continued, saying, "Jesus wants to come and live with you and in you. So entrust to Him your desires and your whole life. Fill your soul with His love that He gives freely in every Eucharist."

"One, two, three, four, five..."

Karol tried to count every candle he could see. There were almost one hundred lit candles. Golden light from the flickering flames brightened the church and warmed the cold mountain air.

Karol tilted his head up. The church ceiling was high and it looked like a summer sky, painted bright blue with golden stars. The prayers of the people and hymns to Mary seemed to drift up to the beautiful ceiling, along with the clouds of incense.

"This must be what heaven is like," thought Karol.

In the distance, Karol could see the golden statue of the Mother of God of Ludźmierz. Mary carried the baby Jesus in her left arm. In her right hand, she held a golden scepter.

Mass was almost at an end, and before the final blessing the priest thanked the people for their visit. Then he walked over to the large wooden box. From there, as was the tradition at this shrine, he spoke to the children saying,

"Mary is your mother in faith," he said to them in a gentle voice.

"So I invite all the children to come to her. At her feet you will see a crown. Your flowers will make it beautiful. With all the flowers you offer her we will crown the Mother of Jesus."

Karol froze. His mother, father, and brother turned to look at his startled face. All at once they all smiled.

"Don't worry, Lolek. Mary knows that you gave away your flower," his mother said quietly. "I saved all of our flowers till now. So here, take these to give to her."

"Oh, thank you, mother!" said Karol, with a sigh of relief.

Then, together with all the children in church that day, Karol walked slowly to the altar. The closer he got the more beautiful the statue of Mary looked.

Father Adam smiled as children took turns to make the crown of flowers. As each child walked away he reached into the large wooden box. Then he placed something small in his or her hand.

Karol waited till he was in his seat to open his hand. In it was the most beautiful thing he had ever seen.

It was a special rosary made of carved rose beads. And it was golden!

"It's time to leave," said Karol's father. "I'm sure everyone would like to stay here a little longer. But it's getting late and we have to return home."

The family made their way back to the town center of Ludźmierz to catch the last bus. On the way, they walked past the bakery and the fish market. Some shoppers carried fresh fish wrapped in white paper. Others held loaves of warm bread under their arms.

"Before we begin our journey back home we have one last stop," said Karol's father.

"And where is that?" asked Karol. He was beginning to feel tired after the long day.

By now they were walking in front of the ski store.

"Well son," said his father. "You will be eight years old soon, right?" he asked. Then he guided his family toward the door of the ski shop.

Karol was a bit puzzled now.

"Welcome, everyone," said the shop owner, Mister Biela. He was an old friend of Karol's father. Many years ago they had served in the army together.

"How good to meet your whole family, Captain!" he said, as he hugged Emilia, Edmund and Karol. Then, with his deep blue eyes he looked straight at Karol, and with a smile he said, "Your father wrote me a letter telling me that you will turn eight soon. And he wanted you to have this."

He reached below the store counter and pulled out a large brown package and gave it to him. Karol could not believe his eyes. One look and he knew it was a pair of new skis!

"Oh, thank you so much," said Karol, as he hugged his parents, brother, and Mister Biela.

"We've had many adventures that I want to write about and draw in my notebook. All the places we've seen, and the people we've met and heard, and the campground, and the golden rosary, and my new skiis!" he said excitedly.

"Yes, Karol," said his father. "But you also know now that the most precious gift we are given is the presence of Jesus. And the greatest adventure of all is our spiritual life."

Then he turned to his wife and two sons and spoke with a twinkle in his wise eyes, "And remember, when we go in a spirit of prayer from one place to another we learn how to live our life as a journey. God does not look down on us from some distant high place. He comes to us as our friend and savior. Jesus walks with us every day on the pilgrimage of life. Let us not be afraid to continue on our journey with God in faith and in love."

Karol now understood that his best adventures were yet to come. His journey of faith was only just beginning.

LETTER OF POPE JOHN PAUL II TO CHILDREN
IN THE YEAR OF THE FAMILY

Dear children,

There is no doubt that an unforgettable meeting with Jesus is First Holy Communion, a day to be remembered as one of life's most beautiful. The Eucharist, instituted by Christ at the Last Supper, on the night before his Passion, is a Sacrament of the New Covenant, rather, the greatest of the Sacraments. In this Sacrament, the Lord becomes food for the soul under the appearances of bread and wine. Children receive this Sacrament solemnly a first time—in First Holy Communion—and are encouraged to receive it afterwards as often as possible in order to remain in close friendship with Jesus. . . .

The day of First Holy Communion is also a great day of celebration in the parish. I remember as though it were yesterday when, together with the other boys and girls of my own age, I received the Eucharist for the first time in the parish church of my town. . . . For how many children in the history of the Church has the Eucharist been a source of spiritual strength, sometimes even heroic strength!

The Pope counts very much on your prayers. We must pray together and pray hard, that humanity, made up of billions of human beings, may become more and more the family of God and able to live in peace…I ask you, dear boys and girls, to take upon yourselves the duty of praying for peace. You know this well: love and harmony build peace, hatred and violence destroy it. You instinctively turn away from hatred and are attracted by love: for this reason the Pope is certain that you will not refuse his request, but that you will join in his prayer for peace in the world with the same enthusiasm with which you pray for peace and harmony in your own families.

Praise the name of the Lord! At the end of this Letter, dear boys and girls, let me recall the words of a Psalm which have always moved me: Laudate pueri Dominum! Praise, O children of the Lord, praise the name of the Lord! Blessed be the name of the Lord from this time forth and for evermore! From the rising of the sun to its setting may the name of the Lord be praised! (Ps 112/113:1-3)

As I meditate on the words of this Psalm, the faces of all the world's children pass before my eyes: from the East to the West, from the North to the South. It is to you, young friends, without distinction of language, race or nationality that I say: Praise the name of the Lord!

Pope John Paul II
From the Vatican
December 1994

About the Author

Jem Sullivan, Ph.D.

Jem Sullivan is a wife and mother, author and catechist. For two decades, Jem has written and taught on various catechetical themes. She has served as catechist and teacher in elementary and high school grades, and as professor at the undergraduate and graduate levels. Jem is the author of books on catechesis, and on Christian art and the new evangelization. She serves new evangelization initiatives at the Saint John Paul II National Shrine, Washington, D.C., and is a regular contributor of art essays in *Magnificat*.

About the Illustrator

William J. Maloney

William J. Maloney is an award-winning professional artist, and retired Art Director of Raytheon Company, who has been painting for over forty years. He is a graduate of Massachusetts College of Art, and has studied under nationally known marine painter Don Stone. Maloney is a member and Master of the Copley Society of Boston, and a Signature member of both the American Society of Marine Artists and the Oil Painters of America. He continues to teach painting, and to bring to life the scenes of Cape Cod, his native Boston, and the places to which he travels around the world.

NEUMANN PRESS

Neumann Press, an imprint of TAN Books, publishes books and materials for children that educate, inspire, and assist their first steps in the Catholic faith.

Neumann Press was established in 1981 by the Dennis McCoy family. The Press became known and loved by thousands of customers for its nearly 200 classic Catholic titles, each one lovingly and expertly printed and bound by McCoy family members and friends.

In 2013 Neumann Press was acquired by TAN. Today Neumann Press continues to publish the vintage children and educational titles for which it is loved—as well as releasing new titles that raise the hearts and minds of children to God.

**For a free catalog, visit us online at
NeumannPress.com**

**Or call us toll-free at
(800) 437-5876**